# I'm learning about...
## The Prophet
# Muhammad ﷺ

SANIYASNAIN KHAN
ILLUSTRATED BY PULAK BISWAS

## Goodword**kidz**

Goodword Books Pvt. Ltd.
1, Nizamuddin West Market, New Delhi 110 013
Tel. 435 5454, 435 6666 Fax 435 7333, 435 7980 E-mail: info@goodwordbooks.com

The Prophet Muhammad ﷺ was born in 570 A.D. in Makkah, Saudi Arabia. His father's name was Abdullah and his mother's name was Aminah. The Prophet Muhammad's father died two months before his birth. Following the old Arabian custom, the little Muhammad ﷺ was sent to spend the first years of his life with a wet nurse. His foster mother, whose name was Halimah, lived in a desert near Makkah.

When Muhammad ﷺ was six years old, his mother took him to visit his uncles in Yathrib,  a place now known as Madinah. It was a long journey by caravan, but young Muhammad ﷺ enjoyed meeting his cousins, playing with them and learning to swim. But, tragically, on the journey back to Makkah, Aminah fell ill and died. Muhammad ﷺ returned home with his mother's maid, Barakah. As Muhammad ﷺ grew up, he was looked after by his grandfather, Abd al-Muttalib, and later by his uncle, Abu Talib.

When Muhammad ﷺ was about 12 years old, his uncle took him to Syria on a trade visit. It was a trip full of adventures. By the time he was 25 years old, Muhammad ﷺ was well known for his honesty. People used to call him "Al-Amin," meaning "the honest one." He was known among the people of Makkah as the bravest and most gentlemanly person. He was a good neighbor, tolerant and always truthful. He always kept aloof from quarrels and quibbles, and never used foul or abusive language.

The Prophet Muhammad ﷺ was employed by a wealthy widow, Khadijah. Muhammad ﷺ handled her business very well and visited Syria to trade her goods. Later, the Prophet Muhammad married Khadijah. They were blessed with six children, two boys and four girls. Sadly, both sons died at an early age. Khadijah was not only the Prophet Muhammad's wife, but also his friend and helper and later, his first disciple.

Soon the Prophet Muhammad ﷺ gave up all worldly activities and set himself to searching for the truth. Often he would stay alone for days in the cave of Hira, near Makkah, to pray and meditate. He would wonder: "What does the Lord require from us? From where does man come, and where will he go after death? What is man's true role in life?"

One night during Ramadan, when Muhammad ﷺ was sitting all alone in the cave, an angel appeared and taught him the first verses of the Quran beginning with the line, "Read: In the name of Your Lord who created…" In this way the Quran began to be revealed by Allah to the Prophet Muhammad through the angel, whose name was Jibril (Gabriel). It took 23 years to complete the revelations of the Quran.

In this way Allah chose the Prophet Muhammad ﷺ as His Last Prophet and Messenger for all of humanity. The Archangel Jibril would come to the Prophet in different forms, sometimes like a man, sometimes like a huge bird, filling the whole sky, spreading his wings from east to west.

As soon as the Prophet received the revelations of the Quran, he would instruct his companions to write them down. The Prophet would always keep one or more scribes with him to write down the divine messages as soon as they were revealed. At the same time the verses were memorized by many companions. In this way the Quran was written down right from day one, and compiled from beginning to end during his lifetime.

When the Prophet Muhammad gave the message of Islam to the people of Makkah, most of them opposed him. Ultimately, the Makkan resistance to the Prophet's message brought hardship and torture to the Muslims. Some of the companions had to migrate to Abyssinia (Ethiopia). The Makkans even imposed a social ban on the Prophet's family. No one was to talk to them or do business with them. This ban lasted for three years, and caused the family great suffering.

One night as the Prophet slept next to the Kabah, the Archangel Jibril woke him up and took him on a strange, white winged animal, called *Buraq* (lightning), first from Makkah to al-Aqsa mosque in Jerusalem and then through the seven Heavens into the Divine Presence. The Prophet looked upon that which the eyes cannot see and minds cannot imagine, the Creator of heaven and earth. This experience, which took place in less than a moment, is called the Night Journey and the Ascension (*al-Isra* and *al-Miraj*).

Ultimately, to stamp out Islam, the Makkans hatched an evil plot to kill the Prophet. At the divine command, the Prophet left for Madinah along with Abu Bakr. The Makkans sent search parties to capture the Prophet. The Prophet and Abu Bakr took shelter in the cave of Thawr, outside Makkah. The enemy came very close to the mouth of the cave. But they left after seeing that a spider had spun a web across its opening and a dove had made a nest just to one side of it.

The Prophet safely reached Madinah, and his journey is known as the Hijrah, or migration. Here he was warmly welcomed by the Ansars, or the Helpers, the people of Madinah. Slowly, almost all of the followers of the Prophet joined him in Madinah. The Prophet's migration to Madinah left the Makkans, feeling cheated of their prey, therefore, they fought with the Prophet at places such as Badr, Uhud, etc. Ultimately, the Prophet entered into a peace agreement with the Makkans at Hudaybiyyah, after which peace prevailed in the region.

The Prophet's Mosque in Madinah became the centre of his activities; he would sit there for hours and hours to give people the message of Islam. The Prophet's message spread far and wide. He sent letters with the basic message of Islam to neighboring kings. Slowly, tribe after tribe began to come into the fold of Islam. The numbers of tribesmen ran into thousands. The Prophet Muhammad taught us that prayer is a way of saying how we need Allah's grace for every single thing we have, and how Allah's power over all things is total. He urged his followers to remember the Day of Judgement, when Allah will judge our actions by punishing the wicked and rewarding those who followed His path. He also urged his followers to spend time in prayer and in remembrance of Allah, and to live kindly and humbly, releasing slaves, giving in charity, especially to very poor people, to orphans and the needy, without any thought of reward.

The Prophet Muhammad's life went through various stages of well-being and extreme hardship, yet never once did he stray from the path of moderation. At all times, and right till the end, he remained the patient and grateful servant of the Almighty, bringing his message of peace and tolerance to all mankind.